If Butterflies Could Talk

Megan Kirchhofer

BookLeaf Publishing

India | USA | UK

Cover by Madeline Larson

Presentation by *BookLeaf Publishing*

Web: www.bookleafpub.com

E-mail: info@bookleafpub.com

ISBN: 9789357446532

First edition 2022

For my high school AP literature teacher: Ms. C, thank you for noticing my pain when I thought I was alone, and for refusing to let me quit writing. I wouldn't be where I am without you. I miss you, and I hope you love this book.

For my younger self: Keep going, you'll get there, I promise. I love you.

Acknowledgements

There's such a long list of people who have supported me throughout this process, and every one of them holds a special place in my life, or marks a special checkpoint in my literary journey. In no particular order, I'd like to express my gratitude and appreciation for the following people:

My siblings, Summer and Noah, for bugging me just enough to keep me motivated and teach me perseverance, but also for always being there and standing up for me in the end. I hope you know that I've had your backs this whole time, and I will forever. Each of you is stronger than you ever should've had to be, and I hope you realize how much light you bring to others. I love you both. (call me).

Mom, thank you for everything. You were the first one to tell me how much I'm capable of, and that became hugely important for my confidence as a writer. I can't even begin to understand the sacrifices you made for our family as I was growing up. I hope this book can serve as a worthy reflection of the person you helped me grow to become. I love you so much.

Savannah and Celia, you both have held me up when I didn't think it was possible, and have been some of the truest, most genuine and supportive friends I think I'll ever have. It devastates me that we're not just a faded-Subaru-car-seat away from each other anymore, but please know that I would cross oceans for you any day. This book wouldn't have happened without your love and support all these years. I love and miss you more than you know.

Grandma and Grandpa, thank you for everything you've done for me over the years. Your endless love and support have been so important to me, and I'm so lucky to have been able to grow closer to you as I grow up. I miss you both so much. Love you to pieces.

Jaden, my love, thank you for being such an important part of this book's behind-the-scenes process. You know me in a way no one else ever will, and you love me in a way I've never believed that I deserve. I owe so much of my health and happiness to your influence in my life, and you'll truly never know exactly how grateful I am for January 2021. You deserve the world, and you have become mine. You're perfect.5, and I love you with everything that I am.

Madeline, you have absolutely no idea the impact you've had on my life, and who I am as a person. Knowing you has changed me in beautiful, irreversible, unforgettable ways, and I'm so lucky to know you the way that I do. Thank you for your art, and the way it made me feel. Thank you for staying in my life, you'll always be absolutely permanent. This book wouldn't have been nearly as full or as magical without you.

Maddy, you're one of the best things that's ever happened to me. Little did I know that the day I met you would permanently alter the course of my life for the better. You mean the world to me, and I can't believe I'm lucky enough to be loved by you. I'll be here for you until the end of time. I love you.

Dani, you're a force to be reckoned with. I don't think you fully understand the impact that your words have had on my life. Your endless support and motivation are truly awe-inspiring. Please keep going. I absolutely can't wait to watch you take over the world. I love you.

Gavin, you're one of the most gentle, empathetic people I know, and the world could really use more of you. Thank you for being by my side through it all, and for accepting me for everything I've ever been. I can't stress enough how permanent you are to me. I love you.

Robin & Shaun, thank you for everything. I'm so lucky to know and be supported by you, even when we're all too busy even to breathe. Your love for each other and passion for living is beautiful, and I'm blessed just to bear witness to it. I love you both.

Louisa, the longer I know you the more important you become to me. Thank you for your acceptance and laughter and foggy April evenings on my couch together. I don't think I tell you enough how much you matter, to me and to the world. I love you.

Ash & Reyna, I'm so lucky to be loved by you both. You mean so much to me, and I'm constantly blown away by your support. You both deserve so much good, and I hope to empower you to demand it. I love you.

All of my coworkers, thank you for everything. I don't know how I'd make it through the day without you. I love each and every one of you and I'm so blessed to be supported by you.

My cat, Peanut. He's just so cute and so dumb.

Dad, we didn't deserve for you to abandon us in the many ways that you did. I don't think you'll ever read this, but if by some chance you do, just know that my pain didn't make me stronger. I did that. Alone. And (no thanks to you) I'm doing perfectly fine without you.

birdboy

I walked my body home
in the rusty, orange dusk
                    —BEING: the
performance of a lifetime—

A Little Boy ahead of me
            found himself distracted by a bird.
                        —the sidewalk blushed
                        at his stamping feet—

He strayed from his mother's hand;;
Her hand hung from its arm
hung from its   shoulder;
she hung from her femininity upside-down.

Upside-down   she dripped a
Masculine into the letters of
                            her son's name::

DRIP.   Bird, perched on a
branch, sings to   Boy (noun)

1

[That's just what birds do]

DRIP.   15 years later,,
a pair of wings stitched by a cell-mate
on the outside of his body.

DRIP.   15 seconds later,,
a command,,   an outstretched arm,,
"Little boys don't fly"   tattooed on the
inside of his body.

DRIP.   For every 0 lost from his
bank account,

                                 one is added
after his   decimal point body.
                    [MAN.000...]

DRIP.   the bird takes flight—

BLINK.   sentences and rust—

EXHALE.   Little Boy™ sheds his
natural androgyny
to reveal a capital letter M

and a lowercase sense of self.

And then the [BOY] tripped on his body;
((ON THE MEANING OF IT))

he fell in blindly,   swiftly,
agreeably,
((THE PROBLEM WITH HIS LIFE WAS THAT IT
WAS SOMEONE ELSE'S IDEA))

but when The Game had finished—
((A WRETCHED, TWISTED SHOW))

he fell out kicking and screaming and clawing at
the ground::

Tally the scores:
BIRD: 1
BOY   MAN   BODY: 0.0000

BOY,   you flightless, featherless thing;
withering, waiting pincushion;
smoking, smoldering shackle.

He walked his Little Boy Body home,
          or Hell, or whatever
                    the difference is.

The rusty, orange dusk
gave way to a deep, indigo skyful of bruises,
and a blackbird storm that
broke into wind

chalk dust

remember when you were little   & you
could spend an entire summer on your hands
& knees in the sun, hands   & face
& shins   & blistering driveway covered in
sidewalk chalk? when you were allowed to just
dump your creativity on the ground   & step
in it   & breathe in the dust   & it didn't
matter that it was temporary?   now it's all you
can do just to sit still in your own body
& nothing lasts but it doesn't matter at all
anyway   & your head is aching with the
multitudes inside of it.   you know you
have something to say   & even more to
feel, but you just can't remember because your
brain is an etch-a-sketch that you can't stop
shaking   & the line between your
daydreams   & reality is a tripwire set for you
at birth.   you can't feel any time
passing but you know it must have done so
at some point   because every time you
look out from your eyes   & down at your

body there's a new stretch mark   & a new

scar   & a new freckle that you

could've sworn wasn't there yesterday.   you

can't fix what you'll never understand   & so

you pretend you were faking it   & call it

your personality, when really you're struggling

          & just can't admit it to yourself. it's all

fine   & good   & normal because

stability is for houses   & boardwalks

          & really tall ladders,   not for the

crashing of the blood in your body

or the collision of your neurons against an

invisible brick wall.   maybe you just

weren't cut out for this.   it's not your

fault but it is your responsibility.

babe, you're a mess   & a fraud   & a

waste of space   & not quirky for

thinking life is hard because   it   just

is.   you can wish all you want for scrapes on

your knees   & chalk in your lungs

          & "special" on your tombstone,

but you can never go back,   so you might as

well draw on canvas instead of roads

& write on paper instead of walls

& read your friends' body language instead of

stories that make you feel real.   because
being real isn't all that   & it's a lot
harder than it looks,   & at least when you're
not really here   & not really normal
then no one will remember when
you fuck everything up.

swallow

My therapist asked me when I first started
feeling anxious.
I don't know, I told her, I've always been this
way.

It always seemed like my incessant thoughts
made me smart—
no one ever told me I was suffering.

She asked about my ~~vices~~ ~~coping~~
~~mechanisms~~————outlets, I told her I
chase my thoughts down the rabbit hole,

squeeze them into ballpoint pens,
and draw tiny hearts on my swollen tear-ducts

just so that when the tears roll down my cheeks
they have the chance of tracing poems along my
jawline.

I've been a writer for as long as I can remember,
and a poet for all the important parts.

My creative process is a spiral—
a hundred thoughts all at once, and all
interconnected,

explode from the flashes of my synapses and
clatter onto the page.
The only clatter I hear now is the reverberation

of tiny blue pills inside their bottle—
my mind is a house that a pharmacist built.

There's a bench at the duck pond where,
when the world is heavy, I like to sit and cry.

I found it one day when the sunset was orange,
and I felt like my lungs were caving in,

and when I sat I found the words love yourself
scratched into the cold, gray stone.

I'm trying, but I never learned how.

Maybe that's what this empty   medicated
chapter really is—

Love in the form of survival by willpower,
not just as a force of habit.

Break,, taste,,   swallow:
I force love down my own throat and hope that I
can stomach it.

Another time, I watched a duck swim in slow
motion,
carrying a bead of water in the crook of its neck.

Oh, to be secure on rippling waters—
to be safe between my own shoulder blades—

that'll be the day I can stop building houses
and start living in my home.

blanket walls

my hands tied above my head and my head
down-bound,
I drill into the center of the earth.

except the Earth isn't dirt and magma, it's the
all-encompassing,
ever-tightening spiral tunnel of my m i n d.

I fashion butterfly wings out of peeling paint on
the tunnel walls,
so I can pretend I'm flying, not falling.

the spiral digs down,   deeper,
darker—
a pitch-black landslide made of putrid oil and
blistering scar tissue.

I delude myself into thinking the fleshy, fabric
sides of my mental corkscrew
are just the plush borders of a couch fort I built
in my childhood, and

I scream through the tips of fine point pens
so as not to blow over the delicate blanket walls
that I,

like a child playing under the covers, past their
bedtime,
built around myself—

it's dark in here too,
but only with my consent.

these butterfly wings scrape and scratch at the
walls as I fall,
slashing holes in the fabric skin of the spiral—

light pours in through the cracks—
a sound like claws on carpet crackles under my
fingernails—

and I see a flourishing garden through the
frayed edges—
meadows of trying and leagues of loving I
missed out on.

finally, I have the strength to catch hold of the
edges and
pull myself through the gaping holes which my
metamorphosis cleaved,

but when my tired body finally lands and finds
respite on a flower,
the petals are paper and it shudders under my
weight.

I look out at where I think an orchard should be
and see
only horizontal blue lines and smoldering soil—

my trauma is an apple tree that never grew,
but I remember exactly when the seed was
planted,

and even though it never sprouted,
the tiny seed decomposed inside of me.

when it had been broken down,
I found it to be a tiny pocket of molten lava.

it bubbled beneath the soil,

cooking the roots of my young, green garden

so that everything new and good grew with
fragile limbs—
threatening to break—   and stained red
with the illusion of recovery.

cartilage—   fabric—   paper —
this apple seed cemetery bears far more
blackness when it's bathed in light.

june.

Would you tell me you love me
on the last day of your life?
Would you take my hand and
lie with me in the grass,
smiling at the sun through the trees
and humming to the song the bright blue sky
only sang for us?

If I lay my head in your lap again,
would you still run your fingers through my hair
and tell me you see me in the sun?

Would you hold me tight
and tell me it was all a dream?
Would you reassure me that the sunset never
ended
and that when I fell asleep in your arms at 3 am
I never really woke up,
and you never really let me go?

forgiven

Forgive me like sleep forgives a broken heart,
Like a deep breath forgives a shuddering lung.

Breathing deeply feels like a privilege— I Toe the
line between wanting and deserving.

I want the love I could never deserve;
Your subtle kindness feels like forgiveness.

Music-filled car rides feel like forgiveness,
You make the lights come on in my vacant
house.

You feed the child that starves in this aching
house—
I can't fail hard enough to drive you away,

You can't drive slow enough to make me restless.
You've watered the peace buried under my
skin—

Tear open my skin, dig up the love beneath,
And forgive my heart for its brokenness.

hex

take me to the breaking point,
where the river meets the sea,
where the horizon meets the sky.
meet me at the middle joint
where Earth's thigh finds her knee
and chain me tight to nowhere so I never have to
die.

strap me to the in-between
with loose knots of unbreakable twine,
as if I'm held but never kept.
tattoo a map I've never seen
behind these canvas eyelids mine
so that when being found becomes a chore I'll at
least know where my body slept.

I call each breath a decision of mine,
being alive an event I chose—
as if control is something that I own—
but when it comes to time, there is no line:
I'm just a boy in witches' clothes,
hexing all I can't understand because chaos is all
I've ever known.

imperfect, but whole

I want to paint the walls of your mind
the softest shade of purple,
and sit inside watching the sunrise
through your eyelash curtains.
Because I love you in the pit of my stomach,
the arch of my spine,
the tips of my fingers.

Because I miss you in the soles of my feet,
the roots of my hair,
the marrow in my bones.

Because being alive is an acquired taste,
and I just wish you were hungry.

I just wish you needed to live
as much as I need you to be alive.
Because if you loved you the way I do,
you'd forget what it felt like to hurt
in the first place.

hemophilia

if roses could bleed
they'd do it behind your back—
quiet and subtle so as not to disrupt
your pretty notion of all you left behind.

it's almost selfless,
the way they bleed in braille—
injuries invisible until your fingers are covered
in it—
but there's omnipotence in the trickling thorns:

Divinity says it's too late,
the blood has been poured and set
into chains that bind you—
blind you—

to your past in ways that don't hurt
until you look back at all the paths you could've
taken
if you hadn't been too broken to notice them—

more broken than you even knew.

the roses never meant for you to notice
how much they'd been cut—
or how deep—
but they're hemophiliacs and they bleed out
every time,

and their life force soaks into the soil and floods
the grass,
chasing the pressure beneath your feet
until you inevitably roll an ankle
and stumble—

if only for a moment,
but just long enough for the rolling crimson
rapids
to wash over your felled timbers
and stain the new skin that you thought you
grew.

and now you're on your hands and knees in the
sodden dirt;
the smell of old blood—
trauma you've forgotten—

shortens your breath into desperate stutters.

where did all of it come from—
I didn't even feel the cut—
how did I let this happen?

but you didn't—
of course you didn't—
because the slashing of these tendons happened
in your soul—
where your nerves can't see—

and it takes a long time for your spirit to cry
loud enough to be seen.

and now the calluses on the soles of your feet
are peeling and cracking
and filling with blood;
all the pain that caught up to you

is now a screen in front of your vision,
tinting the rest of your life
and stamping all your future footsteps
red.

twitches

I dreamt I washed my hair in the ocean and the
salt bleached it white::
knelt in the crashing surf, I whispered my
sorrows to a pinpricked sky.

My skin sang of a grand release.

The echo of an anxious ticking   kissed the
pallor of my blanched knuckles;
phantoms of adrenaline— which once rocked
my wrists to breaking—
fell away in the tide.

The density of a drowned lung   snuck
out from behind these rib-cage bars
and left me with the condensation of merely a
temporary wetness.

These twitches and goosebumps remember
warmth and peace.

To seek shelter from the wind is to sculpt a new
spine of ivy and clouds//
                    twist and bend, fade and
shake—   but never uproot.

—Every cell in your body is dead and replaced
after every 7 years—

::Hush, dear,
let's love you not for old time's sake,
but like you're something someone built to last.

I am not new,
                    only rested.

I am not reborn in the satin tide,
but awoken
            —by the light of a pristine moon
            —by the smell of the life in my body
            —by the understanding that fear is not
innate.

Sleep is deeper in the aftermath//
a chrysalis cracks, oceans sigh, and an unloved body
learns to dance.

things I used to say to my dad that say
a lot about who I've become

"When you're on the plane, can you bring me
back a cloud?"

you told me no.   told me that's
impossible for so many reasons.   because
clouds are just water, and you can't open the
windows.   but I was young,   and in
love with the sky,   and even though you
were right,   part of me wishes you
would've just made something up,   or at
least taken a picture, so I could've just watched
Peter Pan like a kid, instead of criticizing the
fiction.   but that wouldn't be the last
time you forced me to grow up   before I
was ready.

"Can you carry me?"

you usually said yes, and I would jump to the
safety of your back.   I guess I just liked
feeling held   safe, like if I suddenly forgot my
legs, I could still survive.   what no one
told me was that after you set me down for the
last time,   I'd never stop running.
these legs have held more of my weight
than yours ever did.

"Tell me a story."

there's something about the way you spun your
childhood mistakes into comedy routines that
made me obsessed with chasing my youth.
your tales of summer adventures and tiny
failures fueled my quiet rebellion   and
rampant individualism,   but now that my
whole perspective is a journey of overcoming,
it's clear that the stories of your youth   and the
fiction you wrote at my bedside   were the only
true things I ever knew about you.

"Play me a song."

when you would sit with me on the living room
floor and play a song I didn't know on your old
guitar,   the music felt like preemptive
healing for pain I hadn't felt yet. because I was
small   and the world was loud   and I
could sit in your guitar case and feel the
vibrations of your voice wrap around me—
               sure and impenetrable—
      and now 1000 songs on 100 playlists all
compete with the security you packed up the
last time you clicked closed that black case,
whenever that was.

"Draw me a picture."

because the tiny artist inside me was begging to
feel,   to be inspired,   to know what
the world looked like through your wide, green
eyes and rounded fingertips. because creation
has always been in my blood,   and I guess now

I should thank you for failing when you did and
leaving me such   deep   gaps
for me to fill with rainbow colors and fire
metaphors.

"When was the best day of your life?"

I have no memory of an answer, but I know that
the one I always wanted was for you to tell me it
was the day I was born.   because feeling
like I mattered, like I was worth something,
anything,   to you was all I ever needed,
and now I look for that feeling in everything and
everyone.   I can't stop needing to be
important,   and of all the things you've ever
made me feel,   irreplaceable
                            has never been
one of them.

"I was good today!"

I can still smell the rain on your jacket when
you'd come home from work.   you'd
walk through the door, kneel down,   and I
would throw myself into your arms,
searching for a hint of praise or pride in your
face when I told you   I hadn't
disappointed anyone that day.

"I love you."

if only you knew how many other people have
taken your spot at the other end of this phrase.
I like to think you'd be jealous,   like not
hearing this from me anymore is some great
tragedy,   but that would have to mean
that you actually gave a shit   in the
first place.

pandemonium

he spells out "sorry" with the shards
of your broken bones,
dragging them through the dirt on your heart
like a castaway writes
SOS in the sand.

and now he's on his knees,
and he's begging you,
please, can't you hear
the gnawing of his broken heart?

but his apologies taste
like blood in your mouth,
and the look in his eyes
defies the sugar on his lips,
glistening apathy
that foreshadows the continued
snapping of your skeleton.

he cries out for your mercy,
as if he knows the meaning of the word,

as if you were the one to
yank the blistering words from
behind his teeth,
throw your body at his fists;

as if any of this were
under your control.

but there's gunsmoke
in the corners of your eyes,
and you can't fix abuse with flowers,
and you don't have many
bones left to break,

so you pray to the moon
and dress your wounds,
and trade the pandemonium
for creaking floorboards,
an open window,
and a glimmer of a chance
at the rest of
your life.

persist.

and so,
the picture frame breaks,
and the rainbow threads fray,
and the flowers dry out,
but the heart in its cage
still howls at the moon
because
it keeps showing up
night after night;

because
you like how your scars look
in the moonlight;

because
you can only feel your heartbeat
when it's pounding;

because
the damage is done,
but you're not.

if butterflies could talk

If butterflies could talk,
I think they'd sound like a ukulele.
Their gentle strumming would flutter against
the
lawless ringing inside your skull, and
their happy whispers would brush over your
wrists and ankles
with nothing more than the whimsy of
the wind through blades of grass.

If butterflies could talk,
I think they'd speak Latin.
They'd carry the ancient stories that are folded
within the words,
leaving stolen scripture on the petals of roses
and the mutterings of philosophers on the
boughs of forest canopies.

If butterflies could talk,
I think that you'd be the only topic of
conversation.

They'd sit outside your window in the spring,
looking in between the shapes left on the glass
in the condensation from the winter before,
and contemplating the beautiful irony in the
way
you fall apart to the purple glow of
the grow light you bought for your plants.

They'd send notes in morse code
to the girl who sits at your desk,
cheek in palm,
mindlessly drawing flowers in the moisture on
your windowpane.
Her name is Love,
and she's been bored to tears for months.

If butterflies could talk,
they'd be screaming,
begging you to look in the mirror with anyone
else's eyes
and see the vibrancy of the garden between your
temples.

They would riot on your doorstep,
crying about the way the Earth shines when
you're looking at it,
like it's pleading to be captured by your mind
and trapped inside your inspiration.

They'd rattle against your lampshades,
pleading for you to take the negative space left
in your mind
and sculpt it into letters that tell your s-t-o-r-y.
Take the e-m-p-t-y and grow it into something
whole;
scoop out the darkness from in between your
synapses
and shape it into bricks that stack up to your
c-a-s-t-l-e,
and you can sit, and be at peace,
inside the dot of the "i" in your
h-a-p-p-i-n-e-s-s.

If butterflies could talk,
they'd mutter prayers as they flutter around
your body.
they'd read you the potent articles on their
backs,
dripping manuscripts that leave inky streaks
across the petals they touch down on.

Their paper wings are wrinkled copies of
suicide notes written by beautiful girls,
and they tell the stories that catch in the back of
your throat
and hurt to swallow,
but force themselves down anyway.

If butterflies could talk,
they'd be begging you to look past
Webster's definition of your pain
and read between the notches carved in your
branches
by a teenager that fell in love with hurting.

The butterflies are talking,
and they sent me to tell you to listen.
They say the universe is taking care of you,
everything will be okay, and
you are more than the sum of your scars.

let's

let's start a band and be good people.
let's throw sunlight like stones through the
windows of passing cars.
let's burn our feet on the pavement on the first
warm day of the year.
let's feel a butterfly migration in the pits of our
stomachs.
let's write love letters to the wind and send them
sailing on paper airplanes from our favorite
rooftops.
let's call oxygen a joint and stay high forever.

let us remain so vehemently, vividly alive in the
painful swing of silence.

these hands will walk among your hair follicles
and hush you into sleep

and when you wake up,
let's have a picnic in the backyard at midnight.

we'll laugh like we're held together with guitar
strings,
pack illegal fireworks and cheap liquor in our
backpacks,
and scream into wet, pacific sand and
sticky-white sea-foam.

let's please be alive while we can.
let's get tattoos that make us laugh.
let's talk until 3 am, then wake up early to see
the sunrise.
let's sing like we've never heard our own voices.
let's hurt like we mean it.

time isn't real, but we can make it feel like it.
I'll reveal to you my much-ness if you peel
the reason off of your depth.

         we can be infinite if we choose.

let's start a band and be good people.

inch by inch

inch by inch and daydream by silver daydream,
the satin ghosts of your hands   glitter
down my body.

my soul remembers yours
like my wrist recalls buzzing tattoo needles;;

these butterflies are inked onto my heart—

vivid,   stinging,
permanent.

let my skin melt beneath your touch
and my bones become clay—

shape me into the person you used to need
and never got—   I am malleable
just for you.

i'll keep you safe if you keep me real;;
these arms and shoulders will hold you up
forever,

as long as the wonder behind your eyes
stays planted on my lips—   my spine—
          my molten, glowing soul.

peach lemonade

I woke up today in the trenches;
the dirty, cavernous, mud-slung,
smelling-of-blood-and-old-scars,
cancerous, heart-wrenching, heartbreaking,
the dark, the blistering-ly cold, hopeless,
godless, wonderless, abysmal Labyrinth.

My eyes opened, but they weren't really mine;
I looked in the mirror, but my reflection didn't
stare back;
you told me I'm real because I'm loved by you—
I'm real because you yourself are—   I'm real
because feeling like I'm not isn't normal—
I'm real because I know just as well as anyone
how much it hurts to be alive,

but then I blinked
and a switch flipped
and the room between my temples darkened
and filled with Bon Iver and sadness.

I can't tell you how much I want to believe you,

how tired I am of putting gold glitter on my
cheekbones and in the corners of my eyes to try
and pretend I'm made of Sun— made of
something—   honestly, just made of
anything;;

how much I wish I was as real as you say I am.

Real, like peach lemonade—
real like a strawberry moon—
real like the pretty undulation of an ocean at
sunset—
real like the hum of the filament in an
incandescent lightbulb—
real like the birds that swarm at dusk, black
against an orange-purple sky—
real like painted ukuleles—
real like a stomach-full of eagles—

real like suicide notes from beautiful girls—
real like Scrabble letters lost under the couch—
real like the crosshatching of plane trails in a
clear blue sky—

real like dandelions growing from concrete—
real like the pigeons on my windowsill—
real like the eyelash on your cheek—
real like the fingerprints on my poetry books—

real like the garden of stars[night sky]—
real like the illusion of February[too short to be
as long as it feels—
real like the freckles on your shoulders—
real like a fever breaking—
real like the sun through fir trees—

real like the Idiot in the Purple Sweater—
real like the Princess Complex—
real like the Daughter You Left Behind—
real like the Daughter You Never Had—
real like the Daughter I Could Never Be—

real like the burning of my lungs—
real like the anxious biting of my tongue—
real like my bloody nail beds—

real like sugar, real like spice,
real like poems that don't fucking rhyme—

real like broken traffic lights and those assholes
with LED headlights on their cars—
real like cherry wine and crashing planes—
real like the wage gap and America's indifference
thereof—

real like a deep breath after crying—
real like the raw, stinging pain in your eyelids
after crying—
real like the 8 hours of sleep you get when you
collapse after crying—

real like standing fully clothed in a waterfall,
screaming because you can't be heard from the
freeway and the trees don't care anyway—

real like cane sugar and lemon juice and
probably peach concentrate and high-fructose
corn syrup and too many ice cubes and
earth-killing, plastic cups to fill with my
peach lemonade.

Wouldn't that be nice.

Listen, I'm sorry to be so cynical,
but it's not my fault— it's just the whispers in
my head again.

But don't worry:
at the end of the day, I know that I kept missing
my mom
after I thought I didn't need her anymore;

I know that somebody's going to have to take
my laundry out of the dryer after I'm gone,

and right now,
that has to be good enough for "me."

skin

A feeling.   Barely a feeling.
less of a feeling   and more of a moment.
More of an experience.   More of the
motion of a hot breath   on cold skin.
on cold veins.   On veins that bulge
and blue   and scatter and pulse.   Pulse
and breathe   and trip down the
stairs.   and explode on impact. and travel
between   brain.   and heart.
and lips.   and neuron   and
neuron   and neuron.
Do you hear the screaming of the blood in your
brain   ?   in your hands   ?   in your
eyes   ?   Your eyes.   Your eyes say
swim.   and dive.   Deeper.
and deeper.   and darker.   and
holier. and once again,   this time with
feeling.   feeling and motion.
And water over rocks   over knuckles
clenching sand. over aqua-colored salmon
and salmon colored skies.   over

our heads and under our skin.   Our
young, rebuilt skin.   Skin that
tingles   and combusts   and
betrays the rushing   and blushing
of our blood. Skin that dances when you sing
          and sings when the lights go down.
          burning   itching   wailing
          buzzing   glowing
          vibrating   S K I N.
Skin me alive   flesh me out
pick me apart   sand me down
into the pieces of me worth keeping.
worth keeping.   worth keeping and
cherishing   and blessing
and beholding.   Worth everything,

          and more.

crash

call me when it hurts—
when your limbs are shaking   from a
life hard-lived.

hear me sing lullabies
to the sound of your tsunamic heartbeat—

                crash on the rocks,
                        I'll catch you in
                                thesandbar.

you can break your bones if you need—
if that's how you must shed that corporeal skin
                and tantalize your jailed spirit.

don't be afraid of the snapping sounds of your
fraying tendons—
strums on a rusted harp—

music is the conjunction of acoustics and pain—
oceans only hush by the collision of their
molecules.

"you" is a beautiful projection of celestial
introspection.

—and as the universe experiences itself through
your glassen eyes,

    —find yourself not alive, but awake;

      —not here, but everywhere;

       —not ever, but always.

everything-ly, you

The first time I met my lungs,
we were kissing under the stars   in your
car   at our favorite childhood park.

"Fuck— so this is what it feels like to breathe."

I met them again 3 months later
after seeing the top of your head over a wall of
books.
My capillaries expanded and filled with
hot-pink laughter   and the smell of my
chapstick   and floral-tasting weed—
I exhaled the smoke into your lungs
          and that's when I met my heartbeat.

"Finally— you're awake."

It traveled to my palms and danced along the
back of your neck,

then hammered morse desire into the walls of
my stomach
and my naive, shaking thighs.

I turned to rubber and sunk between mattress
molecules,
pulling you down into my lucid,   liquid,
oceanic cavities,
          and that's when I met the tips of my
fingers;;

                    —they didn't speak,
just giggled and murmured
into the folds of your skin—

I followed the road map from your collarbones
          to a sun-soaked steering wheel
to rainbow nylon strings   and
back to the roots of your hair,
and didn't stop to catch my breath

until the bleach dried,
until the acrylic lost its gloss,
until the after-crying itchiness subsided.

and then,
I kissed you with tears on my lips
and earthquakes in my hands,
and you turned out of the parking lot
and into another time zone,
      and that's when I met myself.

The person I am when I'm alone misses
the person I am when your lips touch the back
of my hand
and the corners of my smile
and the crease of my thighs.

You're too tall for my bed   and I'm too
small for the mess in my head,
and the lighting in my Room sans You is the
color of A minor,

      but my sheets still smell like
        your soap
     and my scalp still shivers at your
      name on my phone screen,
     and live photos prove that
    kissing you was   real.

—peach lemonade real
—pink sunset real
—600 mg of ibuprofen real
—winding mountain highway real
—Flesh & Bone real
—quivering January lungs real.

I still have your sand in my hair,
you bright, tectonic, edge-of-the-Earth
daydream, you.

—can I please crash on your rocks?
—can I please wash up on your shore?

You, and your tidal-wave,
super-sonic,   psychedelic,
perfect-and-a-half,   magenta-and-gold,
Hozier-lullaby,   kiss-me-at-a-red-light,
saturation +100,
skin-on-Skin-on-flawless, tingling skin,
1500-mile-wide,   picturesque,
other-worldly, shameless   loving.

You,   everything-ly, you.

57

respirate

Lungs expand—

     the inbound air takes the shape of rose
petals—   an effervescent, pink
gingerness;
     sshhhhh...   the rustle of a
gentle breeze hushes young boys' scampering.
     \ \ \ the stillness of 70° settles
     \ \ \ into the gaps of sky
between tree branches above.
     ^ ^ ^ grass pokes through an old
blanket. ^ ^ ^

Lungs contract—

✳ ✳ ✳ ✳ ✳ ✳ gravity slams baseballs into
leather gloves   ✳ ✳ ✳ ✳ ✳ ✳
dead leaves scratch together,
     sharp edges slice through air as
they fall.

The gravel that turns under passing tires
prays for a better November ending than
beginning.

Lungs expand—

        ~sun~   tints the grass and sky a
satin shade of gold.
Children's jeweled shouts bubble against the
atmosphere;
The horizon is wider than you ever could've
imagined.
        Crystalline light washes over your
shoulders;
                … … … … … … ants trail along
somewhere on the sidewalk.
        … … … … … … … … …

Lungs contract—

Photosynthesis / / gravity / / evolution
Even if you trip on your way
home,
at least you know the ground is
there to catch you.

Exhale certainty for the sake of hope,
\/\/\/\/\/ comb your fingers through the grass
for the sake of sensory contentment. \/\/\/\/\/